Killer *Snakes*

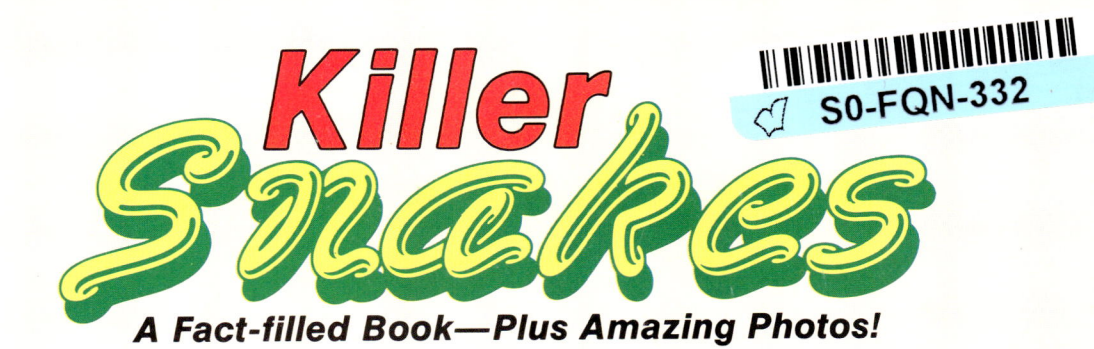

A Fact-filled Book—Plus Amazing Photos!

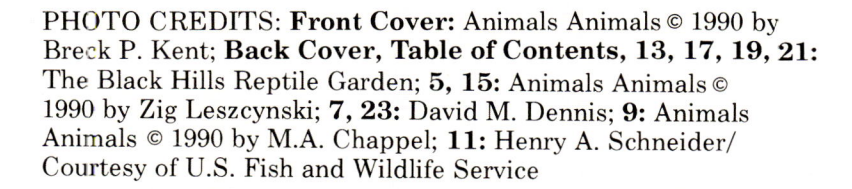

PHOTO CREDITS: **Front Cover:** Animals Animals © 1990 by Breck P. Kent; **Back Cover, Table of Contents, 13, 17, 19, 21:** The Black Hills Reptile Garden; **5, 15:** Animals Animals © 1990 by Zig Leszcynski; **7, 23:** David M. Dennis; **9:** Animals Animals © 1990 by M.A. Chappel; **11:** Henry A. Schneider/Courtesy of U.S. Fish and Wildlife Service

Published by Willowisp Press, Inc.
401 E. Wilson Bridge Road, Worthington, Ohio 43085

Copyright © 1990 by Willowisp Press, Inc.

Based on *A Willowisp Stamp Book SNAKES*

All rights reserved. No portion of this book may be reproduced, stored in a retrieval system, or transmitted, in any form or by any means, electronic, mechanical, photocopying, recording, or otherwise without prior written permission from the publisher.

Printed in the United States of America
10 9 8 7 6 5 4 3 2 1

ISBN 0-87406-443-0

Contents

Indian Cobra	4
Black Racer	6
Rhinoceros Viper	8
Southern Copperhead	10
Eastern Diamondback Rattlesnake	12
Sidewinder	14
Anaconda	16
Cottonmouth	18
Reticulated Python	20
Eastern Coral Snake	22
Snakebite Safety	24

Indian Cobra

Naja naja

- **Poisonous**
- **Length: 4 to 6 feet**
- **Diet: Rats, birds, mice, frogs**
- **Location: India, southeastern Asia, the Philippines**

When something scares you, wouldn't it be nice if you could make yourself look twice as big as you are? That is exactly what the Indian cobra can do.

The Indian cobra has very loose neck skin, so it can flatten the ribs of its neck to form a hood shape. Besides making the cobra look bigger, this hood has markings on the back that look just like another face. This confuses the cobra's enemies, who cannot be sure which way the snake is facing.

Indian cobras are often found living right in the middle of villages. They will bite humans, and their venom is poisonous.

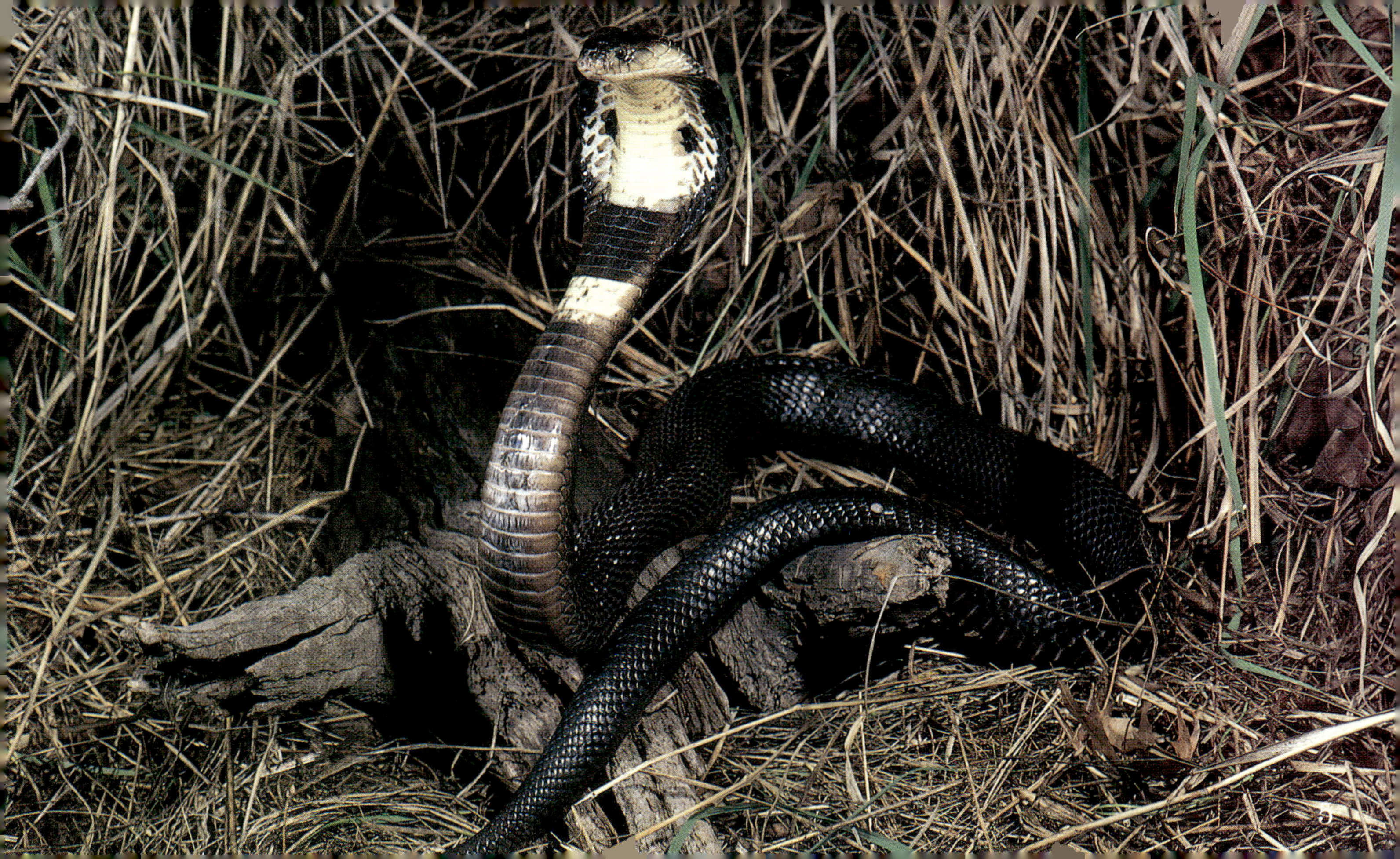

Black Racer

Coluber constrictor

- **Nonpoisonous**
- **Length: 3 to 4 feet**
- **Diet: Birds, lizards, frogs, small rodents**
- **Location: Southeastern United States**

The black racer, also called the blacksnake, streaks gracefully through bushes, trees, and open meadows in search of food.

When a black racer is angry, it will sometimes make a buzzing sound that is like the rattle of a rattlesnake. The black racer makes this sound by vibrating the tip of its tail against things on the ground.

Black racers are not poisonous, but they have sharp teeth and will bite repeatedly if you pick them up.

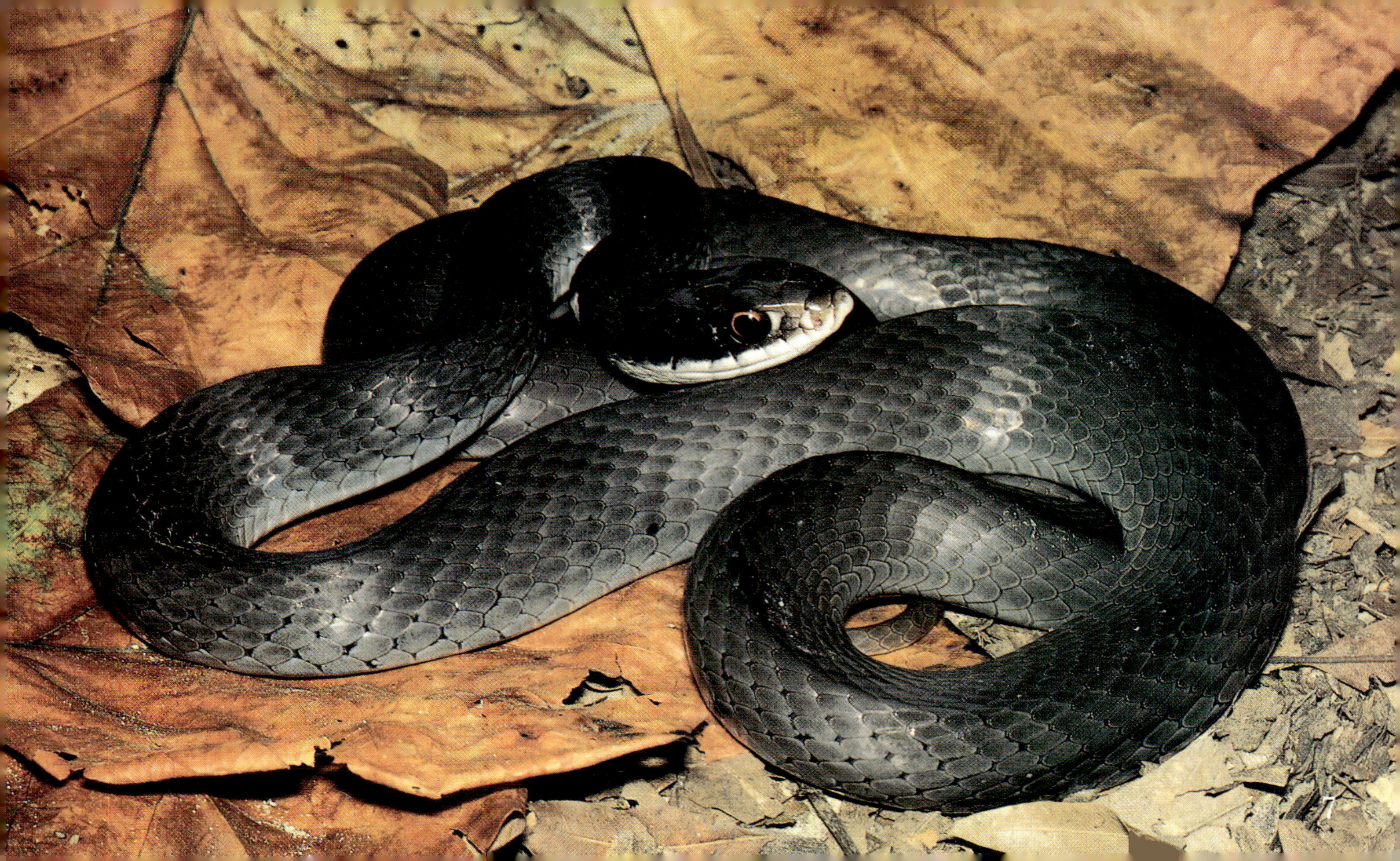

Rhinoceros Viper

Bitis nasicornis

- **Poisonous**
- **Length: 3 to 4 feet**
- **Diet: Frogs, birds, lizards**
- **Location: Southeastern United States**

How does a snake with pointed horns on its head and bright butterfly shapes all over its body manage to escape from its enemies? One way the rhinoceros viper protects itself from its enemies is by hiding in the jungle. It is often difficult to pick out the rhinoceros viper in the jungle because its body markings blend in with its surroundings.

This wide-bodied snake is sluggish in its movements, and it prefers the water to land.

The rhinoceros viper is poisonous and has long, sharp fangs for biting.

9

Southern Copperhead

Agkistrodon contortix

- **Poisonous**
- **Length: 2 to 4 feet**
- **Diet: Small rodents, large insects, lizards, frogs**
- **Location: Eastern and southern United States**

A baby southern copperhead is different from many other snakes because it is born as a completely developed snake. Most snakes hatch from eggs that the mother lays. Without any help from its mother, the southern copperhead survives completely on its own from birth.

The southern copperhead belongs to the larger family of snakes known as "pit vipers." These snakes have pits in their heads that can detect heat. The pits help them to tell when a warm-blooded animal is nearby, even in total darkness. The amount of heat detected lets the pit viper know whether to attack or flee.

Usually, this snake will bite a human only if it is injured or frightened. The southern copperhead's bite is seldom fatal, but it requires immediate medical attention.

11

Eastern Diamondback Rattlesnake

Crotalus adamanteus

- **Poisonous**
- **Length: 5 to 8 feet**
- **Diet: Rabbits, small rodents, birds**
- **Location: Southeastern United States**

The eastern diamondback rattlesnake gets its name from the diamond-shaped markings on its back. It is the largest of all the rattlesnakes.

Rabbits are the eastern diamondback's preferred meal. A rabbit will die within minutes after being bitten and poisoned by this snake.

You will find the eastern diamondback rattlesnake in wooded areas, often hiding under leaves. If you disturb a diamondback, it will hiss through its mouth and vibrate its tail rapidly to make a rattling sound. This rattling means stay away or this rattlesnake will bite you!

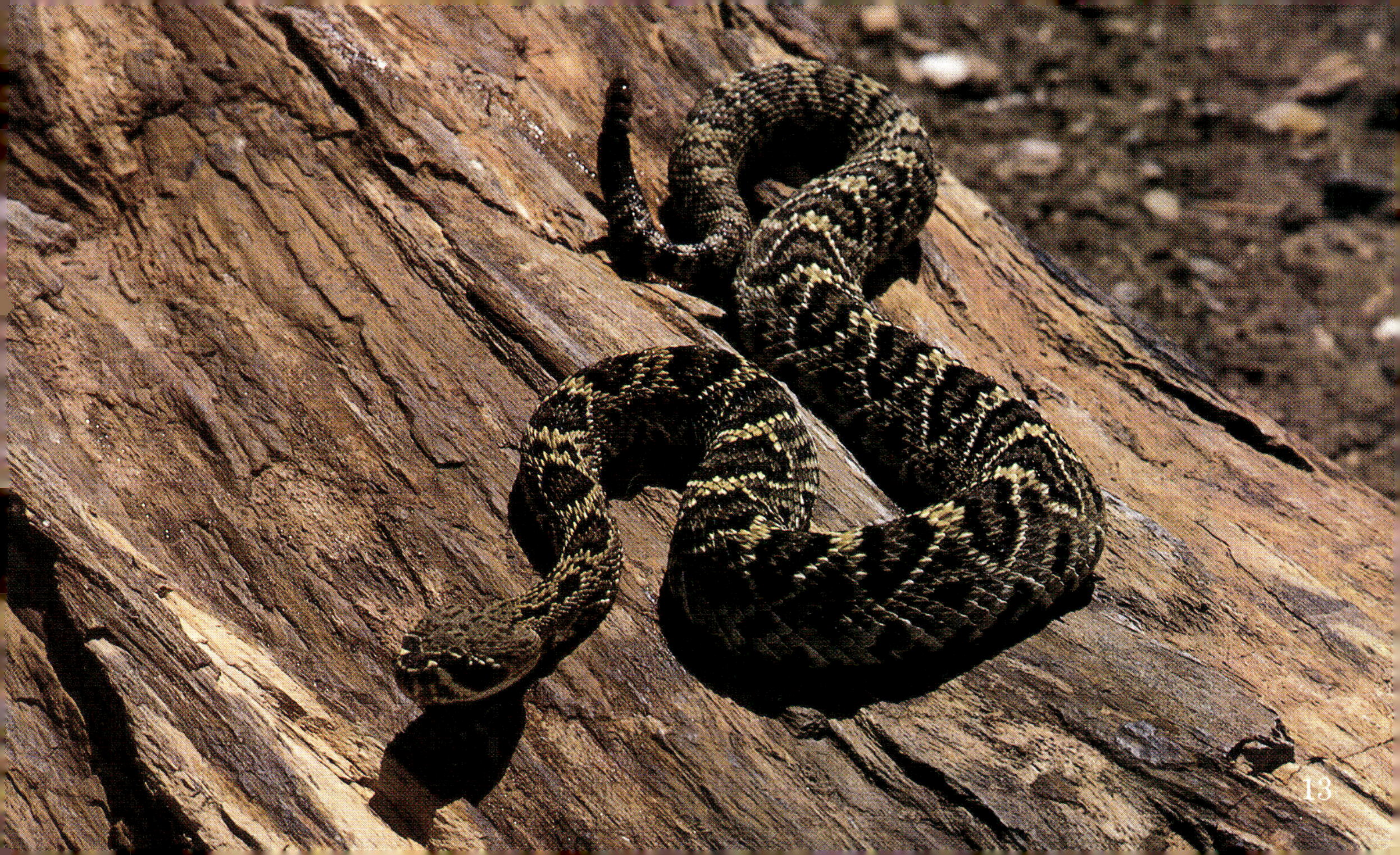

Sidewinder

Crotalus cerastes

- **Poisonous**
- **Length: 2 to 3 feet**
- **Diet: Small rodents, lizards**
- **Location: Southwestern United States**

The sidewinder rattlesnake gets its name from the way it moves. The loose desert sand where the sidewinder lives shifts too easily for normal forward movement. So, the sidewinder supports itself with its head or tail and throws its looped body sideways.

This snake is also known as the horned rattlesnake because the scales that it has above each eye resemble horns.

The sidewinder is a pit viper, and its venom is poisonous.

15

Anaconda

Eunectes murinus

- **Nonpoisonous/ Dangerous**
- **Length: 20 to 30 feet**
- **Diet: Fish, crocodiles, birds, turtles, pigs**
- **Location: South America, Trinidad**

The anaconda is the largest snake in the world. It spends most of its time in or near the water. You can also find the anaconda hanging from trees, waiting to drop down on a passing animal.

The anaconda is not poisonous, but it is very dangerous. Instead of biting its prey, the anaconda will wrap itself around its victim and squeeze it to death. The anaconda is so strong it can squeeze the life out of even large animals! After its prey is dead, the anaconda will open its jaws very wide and pull itself over its victim. If the meal has been large enough, the anaconda can sometimes wait a year before eating again!

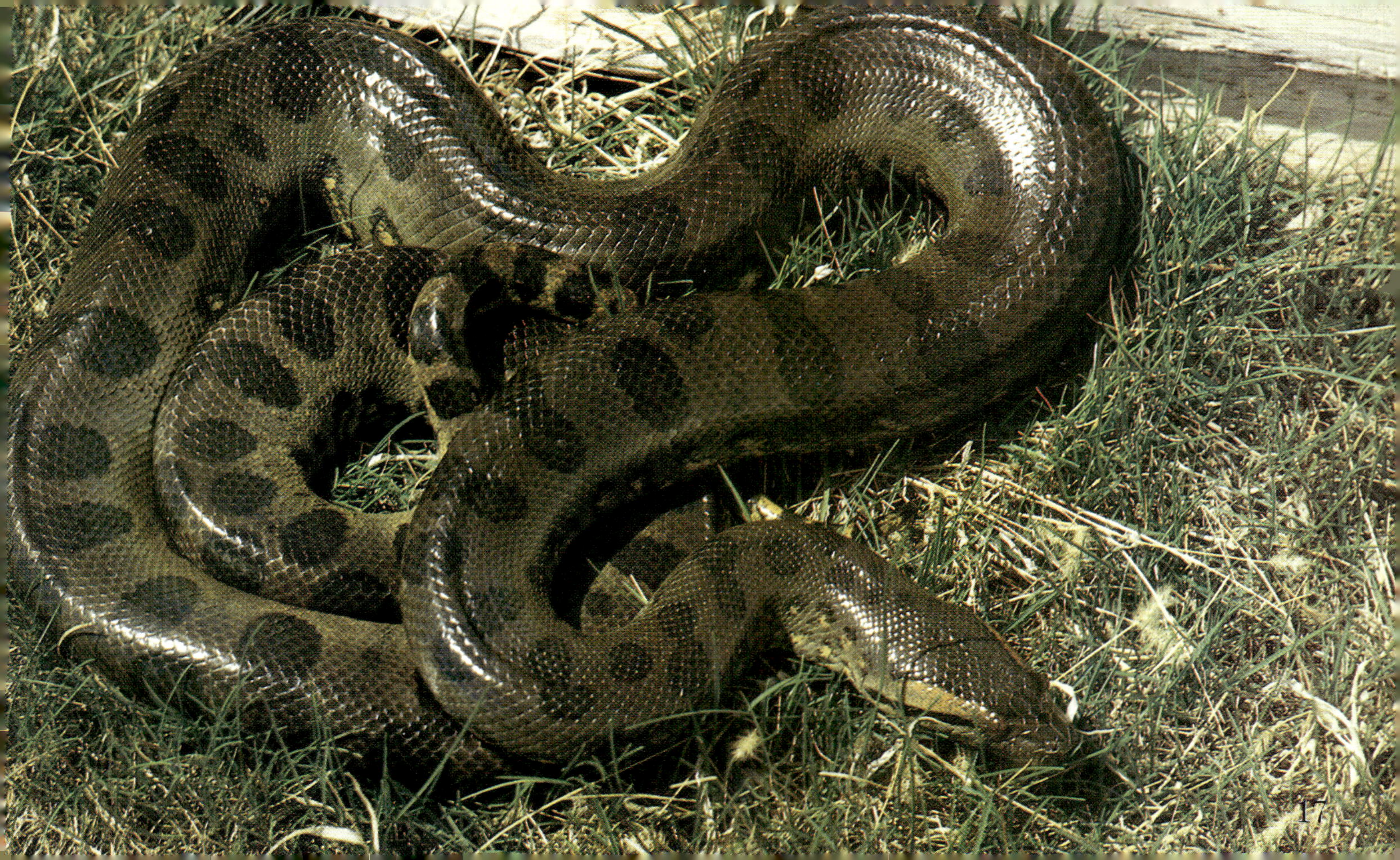

Cottonmouth

Agkistrodon piscivorus

- **Poisonous**
- **Length: 3 to 5 feet**
- **Diet: Fish, ducks, frogs, muskrats, eggs**
- **Location: Southeastern United States**

Don't let the name cottonmouth fool you. This snake's bite can be fatal. The cottonmouth's name comes from the white lining of its mouth. When surprised, this snake rises up, opens its mouth very wide, and hisses. Because the rest of the snake is dark, the white mouth looks very large. This makes the cottonmouth appear quite threatening.

This snake is usually only active at night.

Like the southern copperhead, the cottonmouth is a pit viper. It uses its heat-detecting pits to find its prey in the dark.

19

Reticulated Python

Python reticulatus

- **Nonpoisonous/Dangerous**
- **Length: 25 to 30 feet**
- **Diet: Sheep, pigs, goats**
- **Location: Southeastern Asia, the Philippines**

The reticulated python rivals its cousin the anaconda in length. Both snakes can reach lengths of 30 feet or more! These snakes are longer at birth than many snakes are when they are fully grown. The mother will lay as many as 100 eggs that are about the size of tennis balls. Then the mother coils her body over the eggs to keep them warm. When the baby snakes hatch, they are already 2 to 3 feet long!

The reticulated python is at home in trees as well as in water. It gets its name from the beautiful markings on its skin. The word reticulated means "covered with a net-like pattern."

Like the anaconda, the reticulated python is a constrictor. It wraps itself around its prey and squeezes it to death.

Eastern Coral Snake

Micrurus fulvius

- **Poisonous**
- **Length: 2 to 4 feet**
- **Diet: Small snakes, lizards**
- **Location: Southeastern United States**

Watch out for the eastern coral snake—it is very poisonous! Other snakes will strike quickly and bite their prey only one time. But the eastern coral snake almost seems to chew its victim. The snake attacks its prey quickly and bites it several times to inject many doses of venom.

Although the eastern coral snake generally does not bite humans unless it is aggravated, its bite can cause a human to die within 24 hours if not given prompt medical attention.

Since the eastern coral snake is so deadly, many snakes try to imitate it. The imitators are basically harmless, but their enemies will often be frightened and leave them alone.

23

Snakebite Safety

How to Avoid Snakebites

The best way to avoid snakebites is to use common sense. If you are walking in areas where snakes are known to live, wear long trousers and boots or shoes that cover the ankles. Never reach or step into places you cannot see. This means don't reach up to a rock that is out of sight over your head—a snake may be sunning itself there! Also, never reach or step into a dark cave or crevice. A snake may be napping in the cool air there.

If you do see a snake, leave it alone! Snakes are usually shy and unaggressive, but they will bite if you try to pick them up or poke at them.

What to Do for Snakebites

Think ahead! Know where you can find medical aid if you or a companion is bitten by a snake. If it does happen, the most important thing to do is to keep the victim calm and quiet. Then go get help. Unless you or someone with you is qualified in first aid, do not attempt to help the victim. Wrapping tight bandages around the wound, and sucking on or applying ice to the wound can do more harm than good if done incorrectly.

If you like this book, you'll love *Finding Out About Snakes* and *A Look Around Snakes* from Willowisp Press.